Flirts today will enjoy this
collection of advice and quotations about flirting.
Set pulses beating with your very presence;
a look and a smile can help too - flirting is a gentle
art and will be perfected with practice!

THE GENTLE ART
of
FLIRTATION

Compiled by
Jan Barnes & Beryl Peters

Copper Beech Publishing

Published in Great Britain by
Copper Beech Publishing Ltd
© Copper Beech Publishing Ltd 1999

Compiled by Jan Barnes & Beryl Peters

ISBN 978-1-898-617-19-8

A CIP catalogue record for this book is available from the
British Library.

Copper Beech Publishing Ltd
P O Box 159 East Grinstead
Sussex England RH19 4FS

But give me a sly flirtation
By the light of a chandelier
With music to play in the pauses,
And nobody very near.

Nathaniel Parker Willis
1806–1867

WHAT IS A FLIRT?

A young girl with good spirits can hardly help being a little bit of a flirt. It is very innocent flirtation, after all, and may consist of a side-glance or a swift smile; it is all fair and above board, with no malice or guile about it.

If anyone was to tell a girl of this kind that she was making any man miserable, she would at first be hard to convince, and then be the first to repent and to alter her ways. She is only playing, without the smallest intention of hurting them or herself.

Flirt: - pert, giddy
one who coquets for amusement.

WHAT IS A FLIRT?

She may be flirting in order to secure a particularly good match - or of course, to add another conquest to the list!

Love has no meaning for her. Indeed, the real flirt is incapable of love even in its mildest form, for love brings self-sacrifice and self-surrender in its train.

The flirt remains cool at heart while she plays on the feelings of her victim in her fun.

Flirt: to trifle with, to play
at courtship - to move briskly like a fan.

GENTLE ADVICE FOR FLIRTS

The most successful flirt will be:
a good musician
an elegant dancer
a passable artist
a clever talker
an attractive dresser
a good organiser.

'... a muslin flounce, made very full,
would give a very agreeable
flirtatious air.'

EARLY FLIRTS

In the 4th century, St Jerome depicted a 'modern girl', who –

' ... flaunts abroad with furtive and sidelong glances ... the very ruffling of her clothes is designed to make men look round. Her breasts are tied up ... her waist pulled in ... her upper garment sometimes falls and sometimes tarries to show her naked shoulders ...'

A FLIRT MAINTAINS A KEEN INTEREST IN HER APPEARANCE

Vanity should be encouraged ...

To succeed in the gentle art of flirtation, a keen interest must be taken in one's appearance; vanity, together with a love of adventure, is to be encouraged.

Winking eyes, clacking tongues ...

Passion is becoming a fashion - a falling off in modesty and an increase in levity, the symptoms being winking eyes, clacking tongues, wanton carriage and affected manners. Sleeves are growing wider, bodices tighter and shoes have exaggerated twisted beaks. Maidens, no longer so strictly supervised by their mothers, sigh for suitors and sometimes measure their social success by the number of them.

To succeed in the gentle art of flirtation,
a keen interest must be taken in
one's appearance ...

All the fun's in the fumbling ...

In the days when hoops were worn under women's skirts, men were kept at a respectful distance, but they also served to set his fancies ranging in the mysterious rustling regions hidden from view. However, less cumbersome clothing was on its way and this offered the flirt a different opportunity to catch a man's eye!

'She flirts with him reclining
In a blouse without a lining,
And he's sure to lose his head!'

William Hazlitt, writer, yearned for those even earlier days of the early 18th century when, in courting a young lady, there was room for 'years of patient perseverance, for a thousand thoughts, fancies, conjectures, hopes, fears and wishes.'

GENTLE ADVICE FOR FLIRTS

Madam, you pinch your waist so tight
As to shock all men in their senses;
Your husband still you could delight;
As closely pull in your expenses.
Punch 1873

The head is held a little on one side and
its owner is much given to
tossing and nodding.

The neck of the flirt is often found
to be shorter than the beautiful
long graceful neck.

THE IMPORTANCE OF THE NECK

The flirt cannot ignore this important part of her body. In ordinary street dress, a woman's neck never causes her a second thought; but when an evening bodice reveals the outlines of the throat and neck, it will be wise to pay attention to the texture and colour of the skin.

No woman's neck need succumb to age or ill-treatment. Exercises, massage and careful attention will remedy this vital part of a flirt's appearance.

No healthy girl need fear having to wear a décolleté gown if she goes about remedying any defect with enthusiasm!

A woman strong on
flounces is weak in the head.

I'M A FLIRT

- I -

I'm a flirt, I'm a flirt,
I'm a flirt ready made,
I to masquerades go,
for the gents, it is said.

- II -

I'm a pretty coquette
from the top to the toe,
I'm always admired
wherever I go.

- III -

I've pretty white teeth
and a piercing black eye,
I ogle the gents, always,
as they go by

I'M A FLIRT

- IV -
They wink in return
and I hear them say,
Such a sweet pretty girl
you don't see every day.
- V -
I'm a flirt, I'm a flirt,
o' the real London style,
The gents are enraptured
whenever I smile.
- VI -
There are girls I dare say,
just as easy to please,
But none that can flirt with
the gents with more ease.

'She has two eyes so soft and brown.
Take care! Take care!
She gives a side-glance and looks down.
Beware! beware!
Trust her not, she is fooling thee.
Beware!'
Longfellow

GENTLE ADVICE FOR FLIRTS

'A stubbled leg your suitor will not charm,
And - dare I warn? - no goat below the arm.'
The Art of Love - Ovid

GENTLE ADVICE FOR FLIRTS

A flirt will break some of mama's rules ...
Don't adopt the latest mode
Don't trail your dress upon the road
Don't ever lace your waist too tightly
Don't wear a glove or boot unsightly
Don't wear a thing that needs repair
Don't please, forget to brush your hair
Don't ever show too much of snowy neck.

A LOOK AND A WORD

Repeat his name ...

The flirt will hope to become intimate with men with amazing rapidity! Repeat the beau's name in conversation coupled with a familiar name of your own devising.

This gentle approach, made up of sentimental affectations, is a less dangerous form of flirtation; it eschews the suggestiveness of grace.

Giving him the eye ...

A flirt will develop the art of giving a beau the eye. A timid blush or a 'smile lurking in the half dropped eye' are sign enough that a young man's advances would be welcome.

Flirt: - to run about
perpetually, to be unsteady and fluttering.

Using the melancholy look ...

An experienced flirt will know when to use the 'melancholy look'.

A good plan is to place one or two chairs close to each other in a quiet place. When the 'the object of her eye' is looking at her, she assumes a *most charming* expression of 'pensive melancholy' - this attracts him to go to her side. Her melancholy vanishes forthwith! She has succeeded!

A good plan is to place one or two chairs
close to each other ...

A timid blush or a 'smile lurking in
the half dropped eye' ...

... the flirt will know
the importance of her hands ...

FLIRTY FINGERS

The flirt can talk with her fingers and has been known to make telegraphic signs from the open window to the young gentleman of whom her family does not approve.

The piano flirt ...

At the piano, the flirt will know the importance her hands have in this gentle art. A flirt must have warm and delicate hands.

The piano flirt must be a good musician, otherwise she will play nonsense music all the time she is talking and her conversation will be feeble and unconnected.

The real art is in being able to carry on good conversation over her shoulder as she encourages the favoured man to turn the leaves of music for her.

LAUGHTER

Immoderate laughter is exceedingly unbecoming in a lady; however, the flirt may affect a dimple or a smile, but should carefully avoid any approximation to a horse-laugh.

The flirt should make careful study of the following classifications of 'laughers'.

The Dimplers

The dimple is practised to give a grace to the features, and is frequently made a bait to entangle a gazing lover. This was once called The Chain Laugh.

The Smilers

The smile is for the most part confined to the fair sex and their male retinue. It expresses our satisfaction in sort of liberal approbation; it does not too much disorder the features, and is practised by lovers of the most delicate address.

The Grinners

The grin, by writers of antiquity, is called the Syncrusian, and was then, as it is now, made use of to display a beautiful set of teeth.

The Laughers

The laugh among us is the most common *risus* of the ancients, and is simply an expansion of the smile, accompanied by a slight cachinnation.

The Horse-laughers

The horse-laugh is an undue expansion of the laugh, accompanied with a boisterous noise, and is not allowable in polite society, *even* for the flirt.

Flirtation -
attention without intention.

INVENTIONS TO AID THE FLIRT

The postage stamp ...

The true flirt liked nothing better than to receive a Valentine card from as many admirers as possible. Elaborate printed love-tokens superseded the home made ones and were often accompanied by elaborate boxes of florists' roses.

During the 1820s more than 200,000 cards passed through the twopenny post offices in London on St Valentine's Day.

Even then, Valentines came in three categories - sentimental, silly, and nasty! There was something for everyone at this ideal flirting time - and young girls often sent them to their own sex ensuring that just about everyone received some so as not to lose face!

INVENTIONS TO AID THE FLIRT

The telephone ...

This instrument of Cupid is the perfect invention for whispering sweet nothings across the miles. The careful flirt can have discreet conversations without arousing suspicions.

INVENTIONS TO AID THE FLIRT

The bicycle ...

The popularity of the bicycle ensured freedom for the flirt and one could always topple gently at the feet of an attractive stranger when taking exercise in the park.

Mama and papa will approve of such a healthy occupation - and the young lady cyclist's flushed face will only confirm their view!

Tandem ...

Bliss to the flirt! What could be more exciting than cycling down the country lane and finding a cosy nook?

Coquet - Coquette -
to excite and attract admiration.

What could be more exciting than cycling
down the country lane ...

Gentles take it not amiss
If we give advice like this
Let the flirt none reprehend
Nor importune her to mend
Never chide her, cross nor doubt her
What would parties be without her?

AT A PARTY

In defiance to all steady decorum, the flirt runs headlong into the deepest mazes of pleasure and there carries on her various fooleries.

A party or a dinner is just the place for a skilled flirt who can skilfully encourage the gentleman to cut up her fruit into delicate portions - and even feed it to her!

A flirt will always accept an invitation to a party but she should be aware that gentlemen have been advised to observe a young lady's conduct at the table.

'If a woman tips off liquor with an appetite and exclaims "Good! Good!" by a smack of her lips she is fit for nothing but a brothel.'

'If her jaws move in slow time, if she cannot make up her mind whether to eat it or leave it, she is incorrigibly lazy. Get to see her work on a mutton chop or a bit of bread and cheese.'

William Cobbett 1762-1835

The Wicked Waltz!
'The waltz could be relied on to wake to
wantonness the willing limbs.'
Byron

GENTLE ADVICE FOR FLIRTS

The flirt must be discreet ...
Flirts must never let the cat out of the bag.
Young female friends should never be
allowed to tease or banter you into the
betrayal of a secret.

Trifle - to act or talk lightly;
to indulge in light or silly amusements.

IN THE BALLROOM

Flirtation flourishes ...

Soft music, wine and dancing can help the flirt too!

For the flirt, domestic life, in her estimation, is odious; and she quits the sober and diligent services of home for the flirtings of gaiety, - the opera, balls and masquerades, in which she can display her foibles and be the gazing-stock of the surrounding multitude.

Flirtation flourishes in the ballroom amid a thousand dazzling lights. Flirting is a fever which lives on feasting and rises to terrific heights in the ballroom.

To the sound of music, manly palms touch softer ones, manly arms circle slim waists and eyes flash to eyes sweet nothings.

'The music softens, while the wine inspires,
Disguise emboldens, while the dancing fires
Thence wanton pairs to take a flight
Concealed in masks and friendly shades of
night.'

The mystery of masquerades ...

The experienced flirt will know the value of mystery! Masquerades and other masked balls have always been an ideal place for flirts.

An evening of fun and disguise offers even more opportunity for flirting practice - without revealing your identity!

'Mask'd virgins,
when their blushes are concealed,
Grant favours
which they would deny unveiled,
The power
of blushing, nature's inborn grace,
Will soon forsake a masquerading face ...'
Female conduct - Thomas Marriott 1760

A Spinster's Scheme.

A CERTAIN spinster read one day—
Twas in her morning paper –
A strange event which happened to
The daughter of a draper.

The lady fell into a
stream,
And from her awful danger
Was rescued by the
courage of
A rich and handsome
stranger.

But greater interest than this
The brief announcement
carried—
The lady and her
rescuer
Were shortly after
married.

The spinster thought
some scheme like this
A splendid chance
would give her.
Why should not she a
husband gain
By falling in the river?

She chose a spot at
which she knew
The water would be
shallow;
Then waited for the
rescuer,
Whose life her love
would hallow.

By Herbert J. Brandon.

A manly figure came in sight
As near the stream she rambled;
So, rushing down the sloping bank,
Into the stream she scrambled.

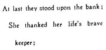

Her cries were heard—her rescuer
Plunged boldly in beside her;
She felt his arm around her waist—
No ill could now betide her.

At last they stood upon the bank;
She thanked her life's brave keeper;
Then fainted as she recognised
The local chimney sweeper.

GENTLE ADVICE FOR FLIRTS

A young girl's head can quite be turned
by the antics of the heroes and heroines in
new fangled romantic novels - so much so,
that she has a defluction of the brain
and a palpitation of the heart at the sight
of every man she meets!

AT THE ICE RINK

The flirt of days gone by liked nothing better than the freedom away from her chaperone when ice skating.

A girl could be gripped round the waist, held tightly by the hand - and be steered into quiet resting areas. Indeed, a flirt could merely slither into the arms of whoever took her fancy - and many young ladies learned the art of balancing on their skates to open up the possibility of romantic encounters.

What we find the least of in flirtation is love.
La Rochefoucauld

A RIDE BY RAIL

A pleasant ride by rail or wagonette is a blessing to the flirt. It is a rare opportunity to have the object of your attention trapped in a carriage for a time - and it would be a flirt lacking in practice who would fail here!

Tempt - to put to trial;
to try to persuade, to entice.

THE CONSERVATORY

A delicious haunt for flirts where they can find a sweet haven amongst the sleepy flowers and plants.

AT A SEA-SIDE RESORT

At evening reunions in hotels along the beach, and on the sunlit and moonlit waves, an exquisite tête à tête offers itself.

Lively Blackpool, with its magnificent high tides and varied amusements, affords countless opportunities to the flirt.

BRIGHTON

"If you approve of flirtations, good dinners
Seascapes divine which the merry winds whiten,
Nice little saints and still nicer young sinners -
Winter in Brighton!"
A Victorian Song

TIMING

Flirt too much and you'll tire yourself and others; practise self-restraint a bit and you'll be a perennial source of enjoyment to yourself and others. Skip a few chances and you'll relish future ones all the more.

The flirt should not neglect any reasonable opportunities but not be too impulsive.

A judicious flirt, well up to the moves of the game, makes them only at seasonable and prudently divided times, using traditional tactics and consequently reaping harvests of delectable fruits!

Always remember, nothing done in a hurry is ever done well.

Dally:
to lose time by idleness or trifling.

PICNICS

The picnic rivals the sea-side as an ideal flirting ground. From the day that the daffodils nod their golden heads in the spring breezes till the woodscapes doff their russet mantles, picnics rule the flirting roosts!

At best, in the ballroom and the sea-side you can only flirt with a few, but at a picnic you can ply your trade with everyone.

'The Springs' at Cliefden is made for the flirting picnic. For there is a famous little pavilion to dine in and to loiter upon and what is especially charming, artful walks by which you can get away from everybody - and boats lying off the bank by the Thames.

Flirtation;
carried on with desire to attract notice.

CHOOSING YOUR TARGET:
HEADS AND HEARTS

The successful flirt will have made a serious study of her target's features; his head, his hair. Before attempting any serious flirtation one look at the man's head can tell you the most effective way to flirt.

A love of good food ...

If the head bulges at the sides, over the ears, this indicates a power for acquiring wealth and a fondness for eating and drinking. This man cares more for a good feed than for literature or paintings.

Fastidious ...

An upside down pear shaped head, with narrow temples will be fastidious about his dress - flatter him. A good book, a good picture, a good poem would afford him more enjoyment.

Sentimental ...

If the upper portion of the side of the head is full it shows a poetical, sentimental nature.

Sensual ...

If the head is full at the base including the neck back and sides, the man is base and sensual, given to voluptuous pleasures and not very particular as to his love affairs.

Stubborn ...

If the head rises to a point its owner will be firm, stubborn and self willed.

Practical ...

The man with a full forehead will be of a practical turn of mind.

Independent ...

If the head is rather flat at the back, the owner will not care very much for family or home.

Entice: - to tempt, to lead astray.

CHOOSING YOUR TARGET:
CHINS

One glance at the chin will offer a clear indication of a man's character, and the accomplished flirt will know how to read the signs.

Crafty ...
A pointed chin is said to be a sign of craftiness, wisdom and discretion.

Sensuous ...
A fat double chin indicates sensuousness.

Cold ...
A flat chin is the mark of a cold, hard nature.

Cowardice ...
A small chin shows weakness, want of willpower and cowardice.

Silly ...

In a retreating chin we see silliness.

Determined ...

A large, square chin indicates a strong and determined will.

Titillate: - to pay attention to, to stimulate gently.

MASHING AND SPOONING

New words for love-making came into the language during the late 19th and early 20th century as courting habits became less formal.

To 'spoon' meant to lie close together, to fit into each other, in the manner of spoons - to make love, especially in the sentimental or silly fashion. To 'mash' was to fascinate or excite sentimental admiration in the opposite sex.

EMPLOY SOFT FLATTERIES ...
'Employ soft flatteries, and words which delight the ear.'
Ovid

Soft flatteries and a startling breeziness of manner are just two more methods of agitating the masculine heart. Only a person with overflowing vitality can develop the high spirits necessary to become a successful flirt.

The table-spoon is a clumsy thing,
A teaspoon is the neater,
But of all the spoons that I love best,
The sofa spoon is the sweeter!

FLIRTING TRIVIA

Sir Isaac Newton was said to have plugged his pipe absent mindedly with his lady's finger when holding hands!

❧

William Cobbett warns against young girls who adorn their body with 'parcels of brass and tin' and other hardware.

❧

A woman without delicacy is a beast; a woman without the appearance of delicacy, a monster! The Lady's Magazine 1818

❧

A flirt has always used all means at her disposal. In 1664 a writer took exception to 'the vain custom now so much in fashion to deform the face with black spots ...'

Young ladies of the time would spot their faces with half-moons and stars to lure the male.

FLIRTING TRIVIA

Watch a girl as she peels a potato; an extravagant girl cuts the peelings thick; if she leaves in the eyes she is lazy; if she washes them only in water she is dirty; if she uses much fat to boil them she is greasy; if she lets them burn she is careless. Leave such a girl; she would not make a man happy.

But if you find a girl who knows how to take a potato, peel it, wash it and boil it, marry her whether she is pretty or ugly, poor or rich; she will make you happy.

At what age should flirting stop?

'At sixty, flirty sexagenarians can be tolerated, but they should think about ending this delightful pastime - a span of time long enough for the most inveterate flirt.'

The amount of women in London
who flirt with their own husbands is
simply scandalous. It looks so bad. It is simply
washing one's clean linen in public.
The Importance of Being Earnest 1899
Oscar Wilde

FINE BRITISH GIFT BOOKS
THE ETIQUETTE COLLECTION - *Collect the set!*
ETIQUETTE FOR COFFEE LOVERS
Fresh coffee – the best welcome in the world!
Enjoy the story of coffee drinking,
coffee etiquette and recipes.

ETIQUETTE FOR CHOCOLATE LOVERS
Temptation through the years.
A special treat for all Chocolate Lovers.

THE ETIQUETTE OF NAMING THE BABY
'A good name keeps its lustre in the dark.'
Old English Proverb

THE ETIQUETTE OF AN ENGLISH TEA
How to serve a perfect English afternoon tea;
traditions, superstitions, recipes and how to read your
fortune in the tea-leaves afterwards.

THE ETIQUETTE OF ENGLISH PUDDINGS
Traditional recipes for good old-fashioned
puddings – together with etiquette notes for serving.

ETIQUETTE FOR GENTLEMEN
*'If you have occasion to use your handkerchief
do so as noiselessly as possible.'*

FINE BRITISH GIFT BOOKS
ENGLISH ECCENTRICITIES

ETIQUETTE FOR THE WELL-DRESSED MAN
Refer to this timeless advice - first impressions matter.
'Only millionaires and tramps can afford to dress badly!'

THE ETIQUETTE OF POLITENESS
Good sense and good manners.
How to be polite and well-bred at all times.

RECIPES FOR GARDENERS
Tried and tested hints for gardeners.

RECIPES FOR AN ENGLISH TEA
Hedgerow jams, scones, traditional cakes,
recipes for removing tea stains from your gown,
recipes for keeping the tea-pot smelling sweet.

MANGLES MOPS & FEATHER BRUSHES
Household hints for the laundry and spring cleaning
from days gone by ...

For your free catalogue, write to:

Copper Beech Publishing Ltd
P O Box 159 East Grinstead Sussex England RH19 4FS

Copper Beech Gift Books
are designed and printed
in Great Britain.